KNIGHTS
AND
HEROES

by John Hamilton

VISIT US AT

WWW.ABDOPUB.COM

Published by ABDO Publishing Company, 4940 Viking Drive, Suite 622, Edina, Minnesota 55435.
Copyright ©2006 by Abdo Consulting Group, Inc. International copyrights reserved in all countries.
No part of this book may be reproduced in any form without written permission from the publisher.
ABDO & Daughters™ is a trademark and logo of ABDO Publishing Company.

Printed in the United States.

Editor: Paul Joseph
Graphic Design: John Hamilton
Cover Design: TDI
Cover Illustration: *Lancer* ©1996 Don Maitz
Interior Photos and Illustrations: p 1 *Far Horizon* ©1989 Janny Wurts; p 5 *Paladin* ©1996 Don Maitz;
p 6 scene from *A Knight's Tale*, Corbis; p 7 knight with sword, Corbis; p 8 *Lone Wolf* ©1984 Don Maitz;
p 9 (top) quintain illustration; p 9 (bottom) reenactor charging at quintain, Corbis; p 10 squires leading
knights on horses, Corbis; p 11 squire dubbed a knight, Corbis; p 12 King Arthur and his knights, Corbis;
p 13 *Lancer* ©1996 Don Maitz; p 14 horse armor, ©2005 John Hamilton; p 15 *Prince of the Lost*, ©1996
Don Maitz; p 17 *Arthur in Battle*, ©1996 Don Maitz; p 18 knights battling footmen, Corbis;
p 19 *Axeman*, ©1996 Don Maitz; p 20 knights jousting break lances, Corbis; p 21 Lancelot jousts
Mador de la Porte, Mary Evans Picture Library; p 22 reenactors fighting, Corbis; p 23 knights fighting in
tournament, Corbis; p 24 knights in combat, Mary Evans Picture Library; p 25 joust on London Bridge,
Mary Evans Picture Library; p 26 knight fights unmounted knight, Corbis; p 27 knight riding galloping
horse, Corbis; p 29 *Arthur Steps Up*, ©2003 Don Maitz.

Library of Congress Cataloging-in-Publication Data

Hamilton, John, 1959–
    Knights and heroes / John Hamilton
        p. cm. — (Fantasy & folklore)
    Includes index.
    ISBN 1-59679-336-8
    1. Knights and knighthood—Juvenile literature. 2. Civilization, Medieval—Juvenile literature.
3. Heroes—Juvenile literature. I. Title

    CR4513.H36 2005
    398'.352'0940902—dc22
                                                    2005048313

CONTENTS

Knights

For centuries people have enjoyed stories about knights in shining armor. Their exciting adventures and quests keep us spellbound as we read about mighty warriors who slay dragons, discover magical rings and grails, rescue those in need, and prove themselves worthy in fierce battles.

The knights that we think of today are mainly a creation of medieval Europe. But other places in the world produced similar kinds of fighters. The Samurai of medieval Japan were elite warriors. Other countries produced great soldiers, but the Samurai had much in common with European knights. They were extremely skilled in warfare, developed a code of honor, and swore loyal service to a lord.

Women couldn't become true knights. Only boys born to knights could undergo the proper training. Still, some women did take up arms and proved themselves on the battlefield. The most famous of these women warriors was Joan of Arc, who fought bravely against the English in 15th-century France.

Some of our greatest storybook heroes were knights, such as Britain's King Arthur and his Knights of the Round Table. When people think of knights, they think of strong, handsome men in plates of shiny armor, sitting atop powerful horses. Knights behaved according to the code of chivalry, always helping the weak, doing good, and pledging undying loyalty to their king and country.

Real-life knights were all this, and so much more. Their lives were complicated and harsh by today's standards. But their adventures have lived on for hundreds of years. Even in modern storytelling, we create characters who hold true to the knightly ideals of justice, fair play, and loyalty. The Jedi Knights of *Star Wars* are just one example of this enduring fascination.

Facing page: Paladin, by fantasy artist Don Maitz.

4

Becoming a Knight

In the Middle Ages, from about 1000 to 1500 A.D., if you owned a lot of land, you were probably a king or a rich noble, often called a lord. In the medieval feudal system of government, kings granted their most loyal subjects land if they promised to fight in times of war. Lords in turn gave some of their land to a group of nobles called knights. In exchange, knights pledged loyalty to their lord, and promised to fight for them. Underneath these two classes of people were soldiers and peasants. They were also involved in wars, but didn't get to own land or hold the title of knight. However, there were certain exceptions. If a warrior fought particularly bravely on the battlefield, a lord or king might make him a knight, even if he wasn't noble born.

Facing page: A knight in full plate armor stands holding his sword. *Right:* A knight prepares to joust in the movie, *A Knight's Tale.*

Knights were very skilled in battle, especially on horseback. It took many years of training to become a knight. Pages and squires were like knight apprentices. They were usually assigned to an older knight who could teach them the skills needed to become knights themselves.

Above: A knight-in-training tries to hit a quintain with his lance.

Facing page: Lone Wolf, by Don Maitz.

If a boy was the son of a knight, he was eligible to train. Noble boys as young as eight or nine started their training by becoming a page. Pages served food, ran errands, attended to a knight's horses, and some learned to read and write. They also learned how to ride a pony, and to fight with blunted wooden swords. Pages had to run a lot of errands, and they were strictly disciplined if they didn't behave properly.

If all went well, by age 14 a knight-in-training became a squire. Squires learned how to ride horses and joust, how to fight with a sword and shield, how to hunt, how to shoot a bow, as well as how to be courteous and loyal to their lord.

One way squires learned to fight on horseback was to practice against a device called a *quintain*. This was a wooden pole driven into the ground, with a pivoting cross arm at the top. A target shield was on one side of the cross arm, with a heavy weight tied to a rope on the other side. Squires charged with their lances at the target shield, then tried to avoid being struck by the weight as the arm swung around. If the weight hit them, it was often enough to knock them out of the saddle. By timing it just right and hitting the shield square in the middle, a squire learned how to attack with skill.

Left: A reenactor at a Renaissance festival charges his horse forward as he tries to hit a human-shaped quintain.

Squires also learned much about *chivalry*, which was a special way that knights conducted their lives. Chivalry was a code of behavior that all knights were expected to follow. It combined military skills with Christian values. Knights who were chivalrous were expected to be brave, courteous, generous, respect women, and protect the weak. They learned to be good dancers, and compose music and poetry. Most importantly, they pledged loyalty to their lord, their king, and God.

Squires were responsible for making sure that a knight's armor was polished and in good condition. They also had to sharpen swords and other weapons. They ran errands, and fed and dressed their master. When a knight got ready for battle, the squire helped him put on his suit of armor. Oftentimes, if a knight got in trouble on the battlefield, a squire had to come to his aid with a new weapon, or adjust his armor, or even fight to save his master!

Training to be a knight was very hard work, and not everyone succeeded. Roger Hoveden, a 12th century writer, once said, "A youth must have seen his blood flow and felt his teeth crack under the blow of his adversary and have been thrown to the ground twenty times. Thus will he be able to face real war with the hopes of victory." The rigorous training prepared squires for real battle, with all its hardships and horrors.

Facing page: A squire is dubbed a knight by his queen.
Below: Squires lead their knights to the jousting field.

If a squire was deemed worthy, by about age 21 he was made a knight. In a special ceremony, an older knight, lord, or even a king or queen dubbed the squire, giving him the title "sir knight." He also received a new sword, lance, and spurs.

In later years, the king dubbed a new knight by tapping him lightly on each shoulder with the broad part of a sword. Early in the middle ages, however, squires were boxed on the head with a fist! The dubbing ceremony was meant to remind the new knight of his vows and loyalty to his king and queen.

A Knight and his Horse

 knight and his horse go together, one working in unison with the other. Good horsemanship in battle was the whole reason there were knights to begin with. To a poor foot soldier on a muddy field of battle, there were few sights more terrifying than a huge warhorse carrying an armor-clad knight.

Facing page: Lancer, by Don Maitz. Below: King Arthur rides to battle with his knights.

In every European land except England and Scandinavia, the word for knight is related to horses. In France, a knight was called a *chevalier*; in Spain, *caballero*; in Germany, *ritter*. These are all terms that come from the word for horse. In England, they used the old Anglo-Saxon word *cniht*, which in time has become *knight*. Cniht originally meant a young man who came from a good family. The word describes the wealthy social status of warriors who could afford horses.

Knights had several kinds of horses at their disposal. A *courser* was a kind of horse used in war. It was specially trained to tolerate the noises and terror of the battlefield, including the smell of blood.

A *destrier* was a heavier horse used by knights for tournaments and jousting. They were tall and majestic, with great strength. Destriers were very expensive, and well bred. A fine destrier signified wealth and status. They were ridden only while fighting. If a knight had to ride a long distance, he used a lesser horse, and had his squire lead the destrier on foot.

Above: Horse armor on display at England's Tower of London.
Facing page: Don Maitz's *Prince of the Lost.*

Rounseys were the most common type of horse. They were strong, like destriers, but not very well bred. They were used for laboring, for carrying things, and sometimes as a warhorse for non-knightly men-at-arms called sergeants.

Equipment for riding horses usually consisted of a saddle and bridle, simply called *tack*. The bridle included a headpiece, a bit, and the reins. The broad reins were often adorned with bands of brightly colored cloth or embroidery.

Medieval saddles had a wooden framework called a saddletree. There was also a seat, with metal fittings, and a covering. The framework was usually made of beechwood. The padding consisted of hay. The outside covering of the saddle was made of velvet or leather.

Stirrups were probably the most important piece of equipment for a warhorse. Without stirrups, a heavy knight in armor would easily fall off his saddle during combat. There is one gruesome account of battle, written by Paul the Deacon in the 8th century, of a knight running his opponent through with his lance, then lifting him out of his saddle and holding him kicking and struggling on the end of it. The knight who delivered this terrible blow could only have done so securely seated on his horse, with his feet planted firmly in stirrups.

Many warhorses were decorated with colorful and flowing pieces of fabric called *caparisons*. Underneath the caparison the horse might have worn leather, or some other form of light armor. Horse armor was rare in early medieval times, until about the year 1150. Metal plate armor was invented to protect horses in battle, but it was so expensive that only the most wealthy could afford it.

It's a ridiculous myth that a knight in full armor was so heavy he had to be hoisted by crane onto his horse's back. In truth, armor was relatively light, not much heavier than the gear carried by today's modern combat soldier. Years and years of training made knights capable of physical feats we would find fantastic today. A knight who couldn't vault into his saddle without touching the stirrups was considered a second-rate knight.

Battle Tactics

When William the Conqueror, a powerful noble from Normandy, in today's France, invaded England in 1066, he brought hundreds of elite knights who fought on horseback. The use of cavalry already had a long tradition on the open plains of France. For the native Anglo-Saxons of England, however, warrior knights were a terrifying sight to behold. The army of English King Harold was composed of about 8,000 men, almost all of them foot soldiers.

King Harold's infantry troops were no match for the Norman cavalry charge, especially in open terrain. The Norman invaders outmaneuvered the Anglo-Saxons and used long spears called lances to kill the enemy. Rows of knights thundered down upon the enemy and crushed the Anglo-Saxons. At the Battle of Hastings, William's army won a decisive victory. Archers and foot soldiers combined forces with the knights and created an unstoppable force. With his enemy soundly defeated, William was soon crowned the new king of England.

In time, foot soldiers learned how to fight more effectively against cavalry by avoiding open ground and by fighting in smaller groups. Adapting to this new kind of warfare, knights also learned new skills. Some knights wore lighter armor and rode smaller horses. This gave them faster reaction time on the battlefield. They were now better able to fight small bands of raiders coming from neighboring Wales and Scotland. These new light cavalry troops were also effective as scouts.

Facing page: Arthur in Battle, by Don Maitz.

Ground troops devised other ways to stop charges of mounted knights. Soldiers from Scotland became experts at using thick spears about 12 feet (3.7 m) long to keep knights away. At the Battle of Stirling Bridge in 1297, a force of Scots defeated an English army led by large groups of mounted knights. The Scots arranged their spears in tight circle formations called *schiltrons*. The knights could not penetrate the wall of spears, which made the Scots immune to cavalry charges.

English armies learned to counter this threat by relying on bowmen. The English longbow could shoot an arrow with enough force to pierce armor. Crossbows were also effective, but because they were slow to reload, longbows were more commonly used.

At the Battle of Falkirk in 1298, the Scots once again used their spears against the English. This time, waves of English bowmen concentrated their fire into the protective circles of the schiltrons. Heaps of dead and wounded Scots lay strewn on the battlefield. Finally, the English sent in their knights on horseback to kill the survivors.

The most important lesson learned from this battle and the Battle of Hastings was that combined forces of knights, archers, and foot soldiers were more effective than any force acting alone. To help support their own infantry, knights learned to dismount from their horses and fight on foot. Other knights stayed on their horses and waited for a good time to charge in. During the fight, archers provided important missile support. This effective use of an army's every strength is known as *combined arms*. It is a military concept still in use today. (Modern armies, of course, combine planes, tanks, and artillery bombardment. The lowly foot-soldier, however, is still doing his thankless task on the battlefield.)

Facing page: Axeman, by Don Maitz.
Below: Mounted knights battle spear-carrying footmen.

TOURNAMENTS AND JOUSTS

Facing page: Sir Lancelot defeats Sir Mador de la Porte in this painting by N.C. Wyeth.
Below: Two men dressed as knights break their lances at a historical reenactment.

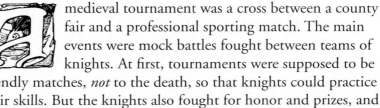 medieval tournament was a cross between a county fair and a professional sporting match. The main events were mock battles fought between teams of knights. At first, tournaments were supposed to be friendly matches, *not* to the death, so that knights could practice their skills. But the knights also fought for honor and prizes, and the "pretend" combat got very rough. People were always injured, and sometimes even killed, at tournaments.

The tournament played a very important part in the life of the people of medieval Europe, including the ruling classes. Like big-league sports of today, ordinary people gathered to admire the skill and courage of the athletes, in this case knights.

Tournaments were held in special open areas just outside the castle walls called "the lists." Local barons or lords first made an announcement that a tournament was to take place. Sometimes a tournament was held to mark a special occasion, like a marriage, or a lord returning from the Crusades.

Townspeople decorated their streets and windows. Knights came from all over the kingdom to compete. They arrived in groups, gathered around their leaders, usually to welcoming applause from the townsfolk.

The Church hated tournaments. A man killed in a tournament was considered to have committed suicide, which in those days was a mortal sin. In time, rules were invented that made the mock combat slightly safer. Swords had their edges and points rounded off, and lances were fitted with crown-shaped points called *coronels*. Weapons that were blunted for tournaments were called *arms of courtesy*. For the most part, however, tournaments in the early days were real fights, with real weapons.

Competing knights were split into two teams. It didn't seem to really matter who was on each team. Sometimes it was knights from the south battling knights from the north, or some similar arrangement.

Once the two teams were assembled, the combat began. Hundreds of knights charged at each other on horseback, using lances or swords or axes to attack their opponents. This massing of fighters was called a *melee*. It was strictly against the rules to attack another man's horse. Anyone who harmed an opponent's horse was disqualified. Harming your opponent, however, was fair game. If a knight was knocked out of his saddle, the fight might continue on foot, using swords or axes.

The general melee soon gave way to a series of single combats between pairs of knights. If a knight defeated his opponent, it was okay for him to help out a teammate. It was common to see two or more knights ganging up on a single opponent.

If a fighter was hurt or tired, there was a special pen off to the side where he could go to rest, kind of like an "out of bounds" area. The rules of combat said it was a safe place. After the knight caught his breath, he could go back into the melee.

Facing page: Two groups of knights compete in a tournament in front of an audience of noble ladies.
Below: Two modern-day knights fight in a historical reenactment.

Above: Knights jousting in combat.
Facing page: A joust on London Bridge in the presence of King Richard III.

A knight-errant was a poor knight who owned no land. (The word *errant* means wandering.) These were usually the younger sons of knights who didn't inherit their fathers' estates. They could also be professional warriors who hadn't won any land for themselves.

A highly skilled knight-errant could make a good living fighting in tournaments. To win, he fought until his opponent was unhorsed, disarmed, or captured. The loser's property (including his horse) then became hostage, and he had to pay the winner to get his possessions back. Losers usually settled their debts on the spot. In this way, a tough, professional knight-errant could make quite a bit of money.

A joust was a part of the tournament. It involved single combat between two knights on horseback who charged at each other. The knights could be armed with swords, axes, or daggers, but usually they fought with long spears called lances. English knights called jousting "spear running," or "spear play."

Jousting was a big crowd-pleasing event. Wooden grandstands were built for the lord and lady of the castle and their noble guests. Spectators crowded around the tournament grounds to cheer on local favorites. Colorful striped tents sprang up where knights could change into their armor. People could buy all sorts of food and drink. Performers such as jugglers, minstrels, or fire-eaters entertained the crowd between matches. Pickpockets preyed on the townsfolk, many of whom were too excited by the tournament to notice. Members of the Church wandered among the crowd, speaking out against the evils of the tournament.

When a knight was called to joust, he mounted his horse on one end of the field, while his foe went to the other side. In the knight's right hand was his lance. It was a plain pole made from an ash tree, about 10 feet (3 m) long. In the later years of the Middle Ages, lances got bigger and heavier, but in the beginning they more closely resembled lances that were used on the battlefield. Lances were tapered toward the head, on which was fastened a fine-tempered steel blade with two-edges, about six inches (15 cm) long.

When the knight was ready, he lowered his lance and tucked the butt end firmly under his arm. The shaft was lowered over his horse's neck, pointing to the left. The knight held his shield in his left hand, covering his left side.

The knight leaned forward in the saddle and tucked in his chin. With his shield held well up, he pushed his feet into the stirrups and charged his horse forward. The two warhorses charged toward each other at break-neck speed, making the ground shake.

Peering through a narrow slit in his helm, all a knight could see was his foe's head, shield, and the head of his horse. As the two sides got close, the knight had to decide where to aim his lance. Basically, he could try to hit the shield or the helm of his opponent. If he struck high, his foe's helm might get torn from the man's head. More likely, however, the lance would glance off. The better shot was to hit the shield square on, which would hopefully unseat his opponent.

At the last second, the knight took aim and thrust his lance forward, rising up in his stirrups as he did so. The last rise and thrust was very important. If the knight made this move with skill and timing, he just might hit his foe a split second before the other knight could strike.

Oftentimes, both sides struck each other simultaneously. The impact was tremendous, even if neither knight was unseated. Each knight and horse weighed about the same as a modern day car. All that speed and mass were concentrated in a tiny lance tip. More often than not, even the most sturdy lance snapped under the impact. If the lance didn't break, and if the opponent wasn't unseated, it was likely that the lance pierced his foe's armor and sailed right through his body.

The knight's horse had to have nerves of steel to run at full gallop into such a fight. In fact, sometimes horses collided during a joust. By the 15th century, tilt barriers were used to prevent this. The tilt was a barrier running the length of the jousting field. At first, tilts were made of cloth, and then they became wooden barriers.

Facing page: A knight on horseback using a sword battles a knight on foot armed with a military flail. *Below:* A jousting competitor races down the field toward his opponent.

KING ARTHUR

Of all the stories about knights that have ever been told, none are more popular than the tales of Britain's King Arthur. For centuries, people have delighted in tales of Camelot, the sword in the stone, Merlin, Queen Guinevere, the quest for the Holy Grail, and many other adventures. Sir Lancelot, Sir Bedivere, Sir Galahad, and Sir Gawain were just a few of the mighty knights who earned their place at Camelot's legendary Round Table.

King Arthur was a warrior king who came from a golden age of chivalry and heroism. Many scholars believe he was a real-life hero of the 5th century. He may have been modeled after Artorius, a Roman-trained British cavalryman who led his elite knights in battle to defeat Saxon invaders.

Stories of his deeds on the battlefield were passed down generation by generation. After a few hundred years, the stories became legend. The most famous written stories are told in Geoffrey of Monmouth's *The History of the Kings of Britain*, written in 1135, and Sir Thomas Malory's 15th-century book, *Le Morte d'Arthur*.

Today, the tales of King Arthur are retold in both books and movies, including *First Knight*, *King Arthur*, *Excalibur*, and the very popular Walt Disney animated film, *The Sword in the Stone*.

Legend says that when Arthur received a mortal wound at the Battle of Camlann, he was taken to the magical land of Avalon. There, the "once and future king" sleeps through the ages, until needed once more to defend Britain from its enemies.

Facing page: Arthur Steps Up, by Don Maitz.

Glossary

ANGLO-SAXONS

The Germanic people who dominated England from the time of their arrival in the 5th century until the Norman Conquest of 1066. Today it also refers to anyone of English descent.

CHIVALRY

A code of conduct, a kind of way that a knight lived his life. Chivalry demanded bravery, courtesy, generosity, a willingness to help the weak, and most importantly, an undying loyalty to king and country.

COMBINED ARMS

The coordinated use of all types of weapons on the battlefield. The English army won the Battle of Falkirk in 1298 against the Scots by making an effective use of both archers and mounted knights, backed up by footsoldiers.

CRUSADES

A series of military expeditions launched by several European countries in the 11th, 12th, and 13th centuries. The main goal of the Crusades was to recapture territory in the Holy Land from Muslim forces, but there were also many other political and religious reasons for the wars.

FOLKLORE

The unwritten traditions, legends, and customs of a culture. Folklore is usually passed down by word of mouth from generation to generation.

KNIGHT-ERRANT

A poor knight who owned no land. Many highly skilled knights-errant earned a lot of money fighting in tournaments.

KNIGHTS OF THE ROUND TABLE

The legendary group of knights who swore loyalty to King Arthur and who lived at the castle of Camelot. The Round Table was a large table where many knights could sit together in a circle. In that way, no one knight was more important than another.

In addition to King Arthur, some of the most famous knights who sat at the Round Table included Sir Lancelot, Sir Gawain, Sir Gareth, Sir Kay, Sir Bedevere, Sir Bors, Sir Bedevire, and Sir Galahad.

MEDIEVAL
Something from the Middle Ages.

MELEE
When two groups of knights at a tournament massed together and fought in hand-to-hand combat.

MIDDLE AGES
In European history, a period defined by historians as roughly between 476 A.D. and 1450 A.D.

NOBLE
Someone born into a class of people who have high social or political status. Sometimes ordinary people could be made nobles by doing something extraordinary, like fighting well on the battlefield. Usually, however, only people who are the sons or daughters of nobles get to be nobles themselves.

PAGE
A young boy who hoped someday to become a knight. Pages began training as young as eight or nine years old. Their main job was to run errands for knights, and learn how to serve others with courtesy and loyalty.

SQUIRE
A young man in training to become a knight. Squires usually began their training by the age of 14. They learned essential skills such as horse riding, and how to fight with various weapons such as swords and bows. Squires were assigned to an older, more experienced knight who helped teach them the skills they needed to learn. Squires were responsible for polishing armor and taking care of their masters' horses, as well as any other errands their masters required. If all went well, a squire usually became a knight by the age of 21.

INDEX